pilgrim

THE BEATITUDES
A COURSE FOR THE CHRISTIAN JOURNEY

Church Publishing
NEW YORK

Authors and Contributors

Authors

Stephen Cottrell is the Bishop of Chelmsford
Steven Croft is the Bishop of Sheffield
Paula Gooder is a leading New Testament writer and lecturer
Robert Atwell is the Bishop of Stockport
Sharon Ely Pearson is a Christian educator in The Episcopal Church

Contributors

Helen-Ann Hartley is the Bishop of Waikato, New Zealand
Emma Ineson is Tutor at Trinity College Bristol and Chaplain to the
Bishop of Bristol
Martin Warner is the Bishop of Chichester

pilgrim

THE BEATITUDES
A COURSE FOR THE CHRISTIAN JOURNEY

STEPHEN COTTRELL
STEVEN CROFT
PAULA GOODER
ROBERT ATWELL
SHARON ELY PEARSON

Contributions from
HELEN-ANN HARTLEY
EMMA INESON
MARTIN WARNER

Church Publishing
NEW YORK

First published in the United Kingdom in 2014 by

Church House Publishing
Church House
Great Smith Street
London SW1P 3AZ

First published in the United States in 2016 by

Church Publishing, Incorporated.
19 East 34th Street
New York, New York 10016
www.churchpublishing.org

Cover and contents design by David McNeill, Revo Design.

Library of Congress Cataloging-in-Publication Data

A record of this book is available from the Library of Congress.

ISBN-13: 978-0-89869-944-9 (pbk.)
ISBN-13: 978-0-89869-945-6 (ebook)

Printed in the United States of America

CONTENTS

WELCOME TO *PILGRIM*

Welcome to this course of exploration into the truth of the Christian faith as it has been revealed in Jesus Christ and lived out in his Church down through the centuries.

The aim of this course is to help people explore what it means to become disciples of Jesus Christ. From the very beginning of his ministry, Jesus called people to follow him and become his disciples. The Church in every generation shares in the task of helping others hear Christ's call to them and follow him.

We hope the course will help you to understand this faith and to see how it can be lived out each day, and that it will equip you to make a decision about whether to be part of this Church. This will happen either by being baptized and confirmed, if this has not happened to you before, or by a renewal of baptismal vows.

You won't be able to find out everything about the Christian faith in any one course. But through the *Pilgrim* course material you will be able to reflect on some of the great texts that have been particularly significant to Christian people from the earliest days of the Church:

- The Creeds
- The Lord's Prayer
- The Beatitudes
- The Commandments

There is one book based on each of these texts in the "Follow" stage of *Pilgrim* (designed for absolute beginners) and one that goes further in the "Grow" (discipleship) stage.

By learning these texts, reflecting upon them, and seeing what they mean for your life, you will make a journey through the great story of the Christian faith. And you will do this in the company of a small group of fellow travelers: people like you who want to find out more about the Christian faith and are considering its claims and challenges.

In other words, this course is for people who are *not yet Christians*, but who are open to finding out more and *for those who are just beginning the journey*. People who want some sort of *refresher course* are also very welcome. In walking with you on this journey we are not assuming that you necessarily share the beliefs that are being explored, just that you want to find out about them.

This course will approach the great issues of faith not by trying to persuade you to believe, but by encouraging you to practice the ancient disciplines of biblical reflection and prayer which have always been at the heart of the living out of Christian faith.

We don't think these are things that should only be practiced once you have come to faith. Rather, they can be the means by which faith is received and then strengthened within us.

Each book has six sessions, and in each session you will find:

- a **theme**
- some **opening prayers**
- a **"conversation-starter"**
- an opportunity to **reflect** on a **reading** from Scripture (the Bible)
- a short **article** from a contemporary Christian writer on the theme
- some **questions** to address
- a further time of **prayer**
- finally, a **"sending out"** section, with suggestions for further reflection and selected quotations from the great tradition of Christian writing to help you do so.

This pattern of contemplation and discussion will, we believe, help you to decide whether you wish to respond to Christ and be part of his Church. Remember that the Church is not a group of men and women who are, themselves, certain about all these things, but who "believe, with God's help" (this is what you are asked at baptism) and then go on following Jesus Christ and continuing the journey of faith.

We all learn in different ways, and there is a variety of material here to support you. Different people will receive something from the different parts of the session according to their own learning style.

At the end of this course, we hope you will have made some new friends and explored quite a lot of areas of Christian faith. Just as importantly, you will have been given confidence to read the Bible prayerfully and critically, and you will have, if you wish, established a pattern for prayer. We hope that *Pilgrim* will help you lay a foundation for a lifetime of learning more about God's love revealed in Jesus Christ and what it means to be his disciple.

This little book gives you all you need to begin this great journey. You are standing where millions of men and women have stood: you have caught a glimpse of who God is, and you are puzzled and curious to know whether the claims of the Christian faith can be trusted and whether they actually make any difference to life.

This book and this course can help you. You will need the book for each session, but outside of the sessions you may want to look each week at the material you are about to study together. As the course goes on, you may want to take time each week to look back at what you have already covered as you move forward on your own pilgrimage.

INTRODUCTION TO *THE BEATITUDES*

Welcome to this six-session course on the Beatitudes. The Beatitudes are a short but profoundly beautiful and influential collection of sayings by Jesus. They sum up his teaching about what it means to live as a child of God's kingdom. They can be found right at the beginning of a long teaching discourse by Jesus in Matthew's Gospel, known as the Sermon on the Mount. One of the ways that Matthew presents Jesus is as a kind of "new Moses." So, just as Moses taught the people of Israel from the mountain after he had received the law, so Jesus begins his ministry by going up a mountain and teaching his disciples.

Alongside other key texts that we are exploring in this course, such as the Ten Commandments, the Lord's Prayer and the Creeds, Christians of previous generations would probably have known the Beatitudes by heart. They were a key text for learning the Christian faith. But in today's church the Beatitudes seem to have fallen out of use. Many people still know the Lord's Prayer by heart and, with a bit of help, most church people can still recite the creed and puzzle out most of the Commandments. But who knows the Beatitudes? When do they get a mention? And what do they mean?

This course believes that following Jesus requires us to engage with this important text, so that it is restored to a central place in the life of the church. We believe that the Beatitudes, and trying to live them out, is one of the best ways of loving God with all your heart and understanding the Christian vision for the world. Like our forebears, we also think it would be good to learn this text by heart.

Here are the Beatitudes as we find them in Matthew's Gospel:

> When Jesus saw the crowds, he went up the mountain; and after he sat down, his disciples came to him. Then he began to speak, and taught them, saying:

"Blessed are the poor in spirit, for theirs is the kingdom of heaven.

"Blessed are those who mourn, for they will be comforted.

"Blessed are the meek, for they will inherit the earth.

"Blessed are those who hunger and thirst for righteousness, for they will be filled.

"Blessed are the merciful, for they will receive mercy.

"Blessed are the pure in heart, for they will see God.

"Blessed are the peacemakers, for they will be called children of God.

"Blessed are those who are persecuted for righteousness' sake, for theirs is the kingdom of heaven."

MATTHEW 5:1-10

In the first four sessions of this course we will look at the eight beatitudes themselves, taking them two at a time. The last two sessions are concerned with Jesus' teaching about living as citizens of the kingdom of God, and then—jumping to the end of the Sermon on the Mount and Jesus' famous story about houses built on rock or sand—consider how we can build our lives on the teaching and example of Jesus, as we see it in the Beatitudes.

In his book on the Beatitudes, *Living Well*, Robert Warren identifies a crafted three-fold pattern to each of the eight sayings. Each beatitude begins with **an announcement of God's blessing**. This is one of the main points of Christ's teaching: God wishes to bless us. God pours love and affirmation upon us. And we are particularly blessed when we live Christ-like lives. Having announced the blessing, Jesus then describes a characteristic that could be referred to as **a vocation**, something that listeners are being asked to emulate or nurture in themselves, such as poverty of spirit or meekness of heart. Then there is **a promise**: this is what the person who lives by this vocation will receive. For the first and last beatitude it is nothing less than the kingdom of God itself. Those who are poor in Spirit and those who are persecuted for righteousness' sake are told that "theirs is the kingdom of heaven." For the other beatitudes some *aspect* of the kingdom is given: to those who mourn, the strength to persevere; to those who are pure in heart, the sight of God; to those who are merciful, mercy for themselves.

In our explorations we will see how this pattern of blessing, vocation, and promise is lived out, particularly in Jesus' own life and ministry. And because some of these sayings are difficult to understand, and quite uncomfortable for today's way of looking at life, seeing how Jesus lives them out himself is the best way of understanding what they mean. So, for instance, if you are not sure what Jesus means by "blessed are those who mourn," look at the examples in Jesus' own life and ministry where he cries out with sadness and anguish to God. This will help us see that mourning is not just about bereavement, but a whole attitude of lamentation and crying out to God when we see and experience the injustices and sorrows of the world.

Even though we will deal with them separately, the Beatitudes are a totality. We should not pick between them, saying we are the sort of person who is more comfortable with one rather than another. This may be the case; our different personalities and experiences do predispose us one way or another. Some of us may find that we are naturally people who thirst for justice or who are merciful to others. But likewise we may also conclude that being pure in heart or meek do not come naturally to us.

Whatever our natural predisposition, all of the Beatitudes are for all of us, and they need to be understood as a whole, and taken as an entirety. They begin with poverty of Spirit, because this beatitude is about acknowledging our need of God and the essential poverty and short-sighted limitations of our own desires. From this the other beatitudes flow. And to some sort of persecution and misunderstanding is where all the beatitudes lead.

They are complex. They are hard to live out. But they are also very beautiful. They describe what it means to live as a child of the kingdom of God, and they are only perfectly lived out by Jesus himself. They describe what it means to live by a set of standards, vocations, and attitudes that go way beyond the observation of rules or the keeping of the law. This is what life looks like when you are truly Christ-like.

In a few short sentences the Beatitudes are probably the most important, subversive, and revolutionary text in the Bible. In order to follow Jesus and live the Christian life we need to enter into the challenging world of the Beatitudes. That is what this exciting little course is all about.

LIVING WITH OPENNESS TO GOD

pilgrim

In this session we look at what it means to live with openness to God and with openness to the world. We start with a provocative little story where a woman who is an outsider comes to Jesus, asking for her daughter to be healed. She is open to God.

Opening Prayers

Generous God, help me to live as a child of your kingdom
Give me the mind of Christ.

Let us hear our Lord's blessing on those who follow him.

"Blessed are the poor in spirit, for theirs is the kingdom of heaven.
"Blessed are those who mourn, for they will be comforted.
"Blessed are the meek, for they will inherit the earth.
"Blessed are those who hunger and thirst for righteousness, for they will be filled.
"Blessed are the merciful, for they will receive mercy.
"Blessed are the pure in heart, for they will see God.
"Blessed are the peacemakers, for they will be called children of God.
"Blessed are those who are persecuted for righteousness' sake, for theirs is the kingdom of heaven."

MATTHEW 5:3-10

God of our days and years
We set this time apart for you.
Form us in the likeness of Christ
So that we may learn of your love
And that our lives may give you glory.
Amen.

Conversation

Be honest. When you think of the Beatitudes, or read them for the first time, what do you think? What makes sense about them, and what doesn't?

Reflecting on Scripture

Reading

From there he set out and went away to the region of Tyre.
He entered a house and did not want anyone to know he was
there. Yet he could not escape notice, [25]but a woman whose little
daughter had an unclean spirit immediately heard about him,
and she came and bowed down at his feet. [26]Now the woman was
a Gentile, of Syrophoenician origin. She begged him to cast the
demon out of her daughter. [27]He said to her, "Let the children be
fed first, for it is not fair to take the children's food and throw it to
the dogs." [28]But she answered him, "Sir, even the dogs under the
table eat the children's crumbs." [29]Then he said to her, "For saying
that, you may go—the demon has left your daughter." [30]So she
went home, found the child lying on the bed, and the demon gone.

MARK 7:24-30

● Read the passage through once.

● Keep a few moments' silence.

● Read the passage a second time with different voices.

● Invite everyone to say aloud a word or phrase that strikes them.

● Read the passage a third time.

● Share together what this word or phrase might mean and what
questions it raises.

Reflection   STEPHEN COTTRELL

Knowing your need of God

What does it mean to be poor in spirit?

Like most of the beatitudes, the meaning is not obvious. Does it mean
that it is good to be poor? Or does it mean that there are different sorts
of poverty?

The invitation of the Christian life is to live our lives in communion with God. This is the way to find fulfillment, peace, and happiness. This is also the way to find riches, though they are unlikely to be the sort of wealth the world holds dear.

Jesus has come to make communion with God possible. Therefore to be blessed—and some translations of the Bible say "Happy are the poor in spirit"—is to receive the blessings of God through relationship with Jesus and by living our lives in the way that God directs.

Therefore when Jesus says, "Blessed are the poor in spirit," he is very definitely not talking about material poverty. Jesus does have a great love for and affinity with the poor. He himself comes to us as a servant. But he also sees the evils and injustice of poverty, and asks us to join with him in building a better world. Rather, Jesus is speaking about the attitude we have to God and to ourselves in relationship with God and with God's world.

Blessed are those who know their need of God.

So you could put it like this: "Blessed are those who recognize their need for resources outside themselves..." (which of course the materially poor often find easier than the materially rich!). Or "Blessed are those who do not take themselves too seriously..." or "Blessed are those who receive and live life as a gift..." or "Blessed are those who know their need of God."

Poverty of spirit is about acknowledging right relationship with God. We are created by God. We owe God everything. God is not another object within the creation, but the one upon whom the whole creation, and all of life, depends. God is the source of life, and God is the one whose endless outpouring of creativity sustains life. In comparison to God we are nothing, and yet through God's great love for us in Christ, we are everything. We are the object of God's love. God wants to make us rich by enabling us to live our lives well. And to live life well means living in relationship with God and with one another. God wants to bless us, but there will only be room for God's rich blessing in our lives (for God will never force himself upon us) if we recognize our own poverty and invite God in. Thus, when we are poor in spirit, when we do recognize our need of God, when we do live in this right relationship with God, the blessing we receive is nothing less than the kingdom of God itself.

> **In short**
> When Jesus says "blessed are the poor in spirit" he is referring not just to people who are materially poor, but to people who are fully aware of their need of God.

For discussion

- Look at all of the Beatitudes and, using the introduction to this course, go through the text and identify the three-fold pattern of blessing, vocation, and promise in each beatitude.

- Put in your own words what you think "poor in spirit" might mean and share examples of when you have seen this in others or even known it in yourself.

Rich in blessing

What will being poor in spirit look like? It will mean recognizing that although we must strive to embody and live by the Christian virtues of, for instance, patience, kindness, generosity, gentleness, and self-control (these are some of the fruits of the Spirit that are listed by Paul in Galatians 5:22-23), these are, as the text for Galatians indicates, fruits that come to us by the Holy Spirit. They grow naturally when we root ourselves in Christ. So it is, again, the attitude of poverty, the recognition of our need for God's gifting and blessing, that matters most. We come to God as ones who are poor and in need. We ask God to give us what we need to live our lives well, and also enable us to persevere so that the fruits of God's richness and goodness are manifest in our lives. Jesus makes this connection when he observes that a good tree cannot bear bad fruit, nor a bad tree good fruit.

"Each tree is known by its own fruit," says Jesus, "for it is out of the abundance of the heart that the mouth speaks" (Luke 6:44 and 6:45).

Because we are poor in spirit we will catch hold of God's vision for the world. This will inevitably lead to lamentation. The world is not as God would have it. The second beatitude is "Blessed are those who mourn," which means "Blessed are those who cry out to God for the injustices and sorrows of the world." The blessing we receive will be strength to persevere and to go on seeking God's will and God's solutions.

But we must choose to be poor in spirit. And we never move on from it. It defines all our relationships. It means coming to Jesus with the same combination of determination and poverty that we saw in the story of the Syrophoenician woman. It means being in touch with the pain of the world. It affects and shapes all our relationships and the way we approach each person, each day, and each encounter. It leads to great joy as well as great challenge, as we enter into the mind and purposes of God for our life and for the world. Poverty of spirit means being rich in God. Yours is the kingdom of heaven.

In short

Being poor in spirit means we live in the knowledge that we need God's help to live lives that are marked by things like patience and kindness, and shaped by God's will. We cannot do it by ourselves.

For discussion

What difference would being poor in spirit make to one or more of the following situations or relationships:

Your relationship with those you love most?

Your relationship with colleagues at work?

The way you pray and the things you might ask for?

Your priorities?

Concluding Prayer

Jesus, lord of time,
Hold us in your eternity.
Jesus, image of God,
Travel with us the life of faith.
Jesus, friend of sinners,
Heal the brokenness of our world.
Jesus, lord of tomorrow,
Draw us into your future. Amen.

Sending Out

During this next week reflect on what you have learned and explored in this session. Think about what it means to know your need of God and be open to God's blessings. How will you let being poor in spirit change you this week?

These readings may help you in your reflections:

> When I began to search for the meaning of life, I was at first attracted by the pursuit of wealth and pleasure. But as most people discover there is little satisfaction in such things. A life oriented to gormandizing or killing time is unworthy of our humanity. We have been given life in order to achieve something worthwhile, to make good use of our talents, for life itself points us to eternity.
>
> HILARY OF POITIERS (315-67)

> If you are wise, you should endeavor to be more a reservoir than a canal. A canal spreads abroad water as soon as it receives it, but a reservoir waits until it is filled before overflowing and, as a result, without loss to itself communicates its superabundant water. In the church of the present day we have many canals, but few reservoirs.
>
> BERNARD OF CLAIRVAUX (1090-1153)

Underneath all the texts, all the sacred psalms and canticles, are liquid varieties of sounds and silences: terrifying, mysterious, whirling, sometimes gestating, yet always gentle. I feel them in the pulse, ebb, and flow of the music that sings in me. As I sing I float like a feather on the breath of God.

HILDEGARD OF BINGEN (1098–1179)

The world ridicules devotion in life, caricaturing devout people as peevish, gloomy and sullen, and insinuating that religion makes a person melancholy and unsociable. But the Holy Spirit, speaking through the mouths of the saints, and indeed through our Savior himself, assures us that a devout life is wholesome, pleasant, and happy. True devotion brings a person to wholeness.

FRANCIS DE SALES (1567–1622)

Unlike the animals and the trees, it is not enough to be what our nature intends. It is not enough for us to be individuals. For us, holiness is more than humanity. If we are never anything but people, we will not be saints and we will not be able to offer to God the worship of our imitation, which is sanctity. For me to be a saint means to be myself. Therefore the problem of sanctity and salvation is in fact the problem of finding out who I am and of discovering my true self. Trees and animals have no problem. God makes them what they are without consulting them, and they are perfectly satisfied. With us it is different. God leaves us free to be whatever we like. We can be ourselves or not, as we please. We may be true or false, the choice is ours.

THOMAS MERTON (1915–68)

THIRSTING FOR WHAT IS RIGHT

pilgrim

In this session we look at what it means to live with obedience to God and with a desire to put things right in the world as God intends. We start with a passage from the prophet Amos about God's desire for justice.

Opening Prayers

Generous God, help me to live as a child of your kingdom
Give me the mind of Christ.

Let us hear our Lord's blessing on those who follow him.

"Blessed are the poor in spirit, for theirs is the kingdom of heaven.
"Blessed are those who mourn, for they will be comforted.
"Blessed are the meek, for they will inherit the earth.
"Blessed are those who hunger and thirst for righteousness, for they will be filled.
"Blessed are the merciful, for they will receive mercy.
"Blessed are the pure in heart, for they will see God.
"Blessed are the peacemakers, for they will be called children of God.
"Blessed are those who are persecuted for righteousness' sake, for theirs is the kingdom of heaven."

MATTHEW 5:3-10

God of our days and years
We set this time apart for you.
Form us in the likeness of Christ
So that we may learn of your love
And that our lives may give you glory.
Amen.

Conversation

Be honest. What do you hunger and thirst for more than anything else?

Reflecting on Scripture

Reading

I hate, I despise your festivals, and I take no delight in your
solemn assemblies.
²²Even though you offer me your burnt offerings and grain
offerings,
I will not accept them;
and the offerings of well-being of your fatted animals
I will not look upon.
²³Take away from me the noise of your songs;
I will not listen to the melody of your harps.
²⁴But let justice roll down like waters,
and righteousness like an everflowing stream.

AMOS 5:21-24

Explanatory note

Worshipping God in the Old Testament involved going to the temple at the major
festivals to offer sacrifices, like burnt offerings, grain offerings, and offerings of
specially fattened animals. This is what is being referred to here.

They also sang songs to God which eventually were collected together in the Book of
Psalms.

● Read the passage through once.

● Keep a few moments' silence.

● Read the passage a second time with different voices.

● Invite everyone to say aloud a word or phrase that strikes them.

● Read the passage a third time.

● Share together what this word or phrase might mean and what
questions it raises.

Desiring the needs of others

The problem with some of the beatitudes is that they can appear to be a manifesto for doormats: blessed are the meek for they will never cease to be stepped on. Indeed, Christians sometimes have the reputation of being a bit weak—so soft that it is amazing they can stand up at all. This is not, I think, what Jesus meant here. Part of the problem is with the word "meek" which is now, in the English language, a much less complimentary word than it was when it was used in the King James Version. The word "meek" evokes in my mind the image of a little mouse terrified at the big world around, that stands just outside its hole looking at the world with big eyes and quivering with fear.

Actually the Greek word could be better translated as "gentle," "kind," or "humble," which might give us a better initial understanding of what Jesus meant—blessed are those who don't fight for their own rights; blessed are those who treat others with gentleness and humility. But we can only really understand what Jesus meant when we read the two beatitudes for this session together ("Blessed are the meek" and "Blessed are those who hunger and thirst for what is right").

Blessedness lies not in fighting for yourself but for others.

This phrase concerning hungering and thirsting for what is right is counter-intuitive. Hungering and thirsting is a natural part of being human and what our bodies do. When we need to eat we hunger; when we need a drink we thirst. We have little control over these sensations but they are what cause us to look after ourselves, to care for our bodies. When Jesus says, "Blessed are those who hunger and thirst for what is right," he is saying that we should seek for what is right with as much zeal and concentration as when we are driven to look for food when we are hungry or drink when we are thirsty. We should allow ourselves to be driven with a desire that is primal and almost beyond our control—not for our own welfare, but for the welfare of others.

This is a good example of seeing the Beatitudes as a whole and not choosing between them. When we read these two together it becomes clear that they belong together. Jesus is saying that blessedness lies not in fighting for yourself and your own needs, but for others and what they most need. Paul had the same idea when he said, "Let each of you look not to your own interests, but to the interests of others."

> **In short**
>
> In these two beatitudes Jesus is not asking us all to be wishy-washy, but to be people who gently but insistently fight for justice for those around us.

For discussion

Who do you think are good examples of people who hunger and thirst for what is right? Share stories of people who have inspired you with their yearning for justice in the world.

Amos calls for justice and righteousness to flow, and some translations of these beatitudes translate "what is right" as "righteousness." What do you think justice and righteousness are?

Can you think of an example of something you might do differently if you were to take these beatitudes to heart?

Standing against what is wrong

The more you think about it, the clearer it is that it is hard for a "doormat" to hunger and thirst for what is right. People who hunger and thirst for what is right cannot help but run into conflict with those whose interests are tied up in what is *not* right. Jesus himself is a good example of this since his yearning for what is right led him into direct conflict with the authorities of his day.

Often, when people cite Christian meekness they also use a phrase from slightly later in the Sermon on the Mount: "If anyone strikes you on the right cheek, turn the other also" (Matthew 5:39). Various commentators on this passage have questioned whether we have through the years misunderstood what Jesus was saying here. If you hit someone on their right cheek, you have to use either the back of your right hand or your left hand. Either of these was the sign of the most profound disrespect. Turning the other cheek would insist on them striking you with their right hand as an equal. If this is true, then what Jesus might have meant here was that his followers should stand up to those who oppress them (and others) with a quiet dignity. Turning the other cheek is not a giving-in to bullies but, with a spirit like that of Jesus who faced death with gentle dignity, it is a quiet standing-up to all those who seek to oppress, and insisting that we—and those for whom we seek justice—be treated with dignity and respect.

> **In short**
>
> Hungering and thirsting for what is right can mean that we end up in conflict with those whose interests are tied up in what is not right. Jesus calls us to stand up with gentle dignity to those people and to continue to call for justice.

For discussion

- Do you think the word "meek" is a good one here? (No pressure, you can if you like!) What other words or phrases might we use instead/alongside it to capture the ideas of these two beatitudes. Spend some time playing with some possibilities (for example, "Blessed are those who gently insist on the rights of others...").

- In today's world, what might "turning the other cheek" mean in practice?

Concluding Prayer

Jesus, lord of time,
Hold us in your eternity.
Jesus, image of God,
Travel with us the life of faith.
Jesus, friend of sinners,
Heal the brokenness of our world.
Jesus, lord of tomorrow,
Draw us into your future. Amen.

Sending Out

During this next week reflect on what you have learned and explored in this session. Think about the word "meek" and how it may apply to you; and also ask God to give you a heart that thirsts for justice and righteousness, and think about how this might be manifest in your life. Are there things you could be more involved with, such as Episcopal Relief and Development, that would give expression to this hunger?

These readings may help you in your reflections:

> Listen carefully, my child, to the instructions of your teacher, and attend with the ear of your heart to the advice of a loving father. Welcome it and faithfully put it into practice; so that through the labor of obedience you may return to God from whom you have drifted through the sloth of disobedience. To you, whomever you may be, are my words addressed that, renouncing your own will and taking up the strong and glorious weapons of obedience, you may do battle in the service of Christ the Lord, our true King.
>
> BENEDICT (480-550)

> It seems very easy to say that we will surrender our will to someone until we try it and find that it is much the hardest thing we can do

if we carry it out fully. The Lord knows what each of us can bear in this regard and, when God sees that one of us is strong, he does not hesitate to fulfill his will in us. For my own part, I believe that love is the measure of our ability to bear crosses, whether great or small.

TERESA OF AVILA (1515–82)

Every act of obedience is an approach to God.

JOHN HENRY NEWMAN (1801–90)

Too often when we bring a message, people perceive us and the message which comes through us separately because we are not sufficiently identified with what we have got to say. In order to be identified we must so read the gospel, make it so much ourselves, and ourselves so much the gospel, that when we speak from within it, in its name, it should be simply whatever words we use. I am not speaking of quotations: it should be simply the gospel that speaks and we should be like a voice—God's voice.

METROPOLITAN ANTHONY OF SOUROZH (1914–2003)

We know we have found our vocation when we stop thinking about how to live and begin to live.

THOMAS MERTON (1915–68)

When a crisis occurs I may find in myself the sheer moral impossibility of obeying God. It is not simply a matter of emotional rebellion, or of knowing that the "spirit is willing but the flesh is weak"; the will itself is unwilling. I am rebellious to the core and do not even want to want God's will. I am helpless; and as the father of the epileptic boy cried to Jesus, "I do believe, help my unbelief," so I too can only say to God, "I am rebellious down to my roots; help me."

MARIA BOULDING (1929–2009)

LIVING TRANSPARENTLY

pilgrim

In this session we look at what it means to show others the mercy God freely gives to us and to strive to be transparent in all we do and are. We begin with Jesus' disturbing little story about a man who is forgiven himself, but cannot forgive others.

Opening Prayers

Generous God, help me to live as a child of your kingdom
Give me the mind of Christ.

Let us hear our Lord's blessing on those who follow him.

"Blessed are the poor in spirit, for theirs is the kingdom of heaven.
"Blessed are those who mourn, for they will be comforted.
"Blessed are the meek, for they will inherit the earth.
"Blessed are those who hunger and thirst for righteousness, for they will be filled.
"Blessed are the merciful, for they will receive mercy.
"Blessed are the pure in heart, for they will see God.
"Blessed are the peacemakers, for they will be called children of God.
"Blessed are those who are persecuted for righteousness' sake, for theirs is the kingdom of heaven."

MATTHEW 5:3-10

God of our days and years
We set this time apart for you.
Form us in the likeness of Christ
So that we may learn of your love
And that our lives may give you glory.
Amen.

Conversation

We are halfway through the Beatitudes. Why, in your opinion, are they so puzzling and so difficult? Have our explorations so far changed or influenced how you react or live in daily life?

Reflecting on Scripture

Reading

"For this reason the kingdom of heaven may be compared to a king who wished to settle accounts with his slaves. [24]When he began the reckoning, one who owed him ten thousand talents was brought to him; [25]and, as he could not pay, his lord ordered him to be sold, together with his wife and children and all his possessions, and payment to be made. [26]So the slave fell on his knees before him, saying, 'Have patience with me, and I will pay you everything.' [27]And out of pity for him, the lord of that slave released him and forgave him the debt. [28]But that same slave, as he went out, came upon one of his fellow slaves who owed him a hundred denarii; and seizing him by the throat, he said, 'Pay what you owe.' [29]Then his fellow slave fell down and pleaded with him, 'Have patience with me, and I will pay you.' [30]But he refused; then he went and threw him into prison until he should pay the debt. [31]When his fellow slaves saw what had happened, they were greatly distressed, and they went and reported to their lord all that had taken place. [32]Then his lord summoned him and said to him, 'You wicked slave! I forgave you all that debt because you pleaded with me. [33]Should you not have had mercy on your fellow slave, as I had mercy on you?' [34]And in anger his lord handed him over to be tortured until he should pay his entire debt. [35]So my heavenly Father will also do to every one of you, if you do not forgive your brother or sister from your heart."

MATTHEW 18:23-35

Explanatory note

A talent, such as is mentioned here, is a large monetary measure equal to around 6,000 denarii. To owe someone "ten thousand talents" was a very large debt indeed. (One denarius is often said to be the equivalent of a day's wage.)

- Read the passage through once.
- Keep a few moments' silence.
- Read the passage a second time with different voices.
- Invite everyone to say aloud a word or phrase that strikes them.
- Read the passage a third time.
- Share together what this word or phrase might mean and what questions it raises.

Reflection

Blessed are the pure in heart

Over the centuries the church has identified certain ways of behaving that are destructive. There are things that we all do which not only diminish others, but which harm us in the process. Ultimately, if we get locked into acting in these ways we end up destroying relationships. It's why they're called "deadly sins." The term comes from the Bible. The first letter of John speaks of "the sin that is deadly" (1 John 5:16-18).

Traditionally, there are seven deadly sins. Pride has always been considered the first and worst sin. It's said that it was pride that prompted Adam to disobey God and pick "the fruit of the tree of knowledge of good and evil." There is a good side to pride; for example, taking pride in one's appearance. Not to do so may be a sign of poor self-esteem. But pride becomes deadly when it leads us to think that we are better than others and always right. The sin of greed alerts us to the danger of never being content. We fail to recognize the good things that we enjoy, and when we get what we are aiming for we don't get happier, we just want more. Then there is lust (the sin everyone remembers), sloth (the one that everyone forgets), and gluttony (the one we all enjoy). Finally, this ancient wisdom names two things that can be particularly destructive: anger and envy.

We call them "deadly sins," but they are better termed "deadly motives." Taken together, they form a guide to help us untangle our desires. They help us identify the good from the not so good, and to spot what is destructive before too much damage is done. Why do we do the things that we do? What is driving us? These are questions we each need to wrestle with if we are to grow in personal integrity and live transparently.

Life is complex, and we all have mixed motives. Our loving, even in the best of us, can be shot through with selfishness. It is why Jesus taught his disciples, "Blessed are the pure in heart, for they shall see God." When we pray for purity of heart we allow God access to our inner conflicts so that God can help us. The struggle is lifelong. In the words of Paul, "For now we see in a mirror, dimly, but then we will see face to face" (1 Corinthians 13:12). We are sustained not only by God's grace but by the prospect that one day we shall see God face to face. Seeing God is our final destination, our ultimate happiness, our spiritual homecoming. But it will also be a day of reckoning for humankind because before God there is total transparency. Again in the words of Paul, God "will bring to light things now hidden in darkness and disclose the secret purposes of the heart" (1 Corinthians 4:5).

> **In short**
> Praying for purity of heart is a prayer that God will untangle our complex inner conflicts so that we can, one day, stand and look at God face to face.

For discussion

Jesus' call for "purity of heart" provokes questions about personal integrity. Are there issues I'm not facing? Am I living in accord with my conscience? How transparent am I in my dealings with others?

If you were to list today's "seven deadly sins," what would they be?

Blessed are the merciful

Mercy is not a popular virtue in a culture of self-assertiveness. But the journey Jesus invites us to make in his company includes the transformation of our relationships. It is a journey from opaqueness to transparency in the way we treat others. "Blessed are the merciful," he says, "for they shall receive mercy." Mercy reaches beyond mere toleration to forgiveness and acceptance.

In the medieval Church, drawing upon Jesus' teaching in Matthew 25:34-46, Christians identified "seven corporal acts of mercy" as an antidote to the "seven deadly sins." There are things we can all do in our service of others that interrupt our tendency to self-obsession and open us up to God. We have choices in life and our medieval forebears identified seven practical ways in which we can show mercy: feeding the hungry, giving drink to the thirsty, clothing the destitute, housing the homeless, visiting the sick, supporting prisoners, and burying the dead.

We cannot always choose what we *feel* about people or situations, but we can choose what we *do*, what we *say*, and *how we say it*. Jesus Christ invites us not only to pray for purity of heart, but also for the grace to re-order our lives and priorities so that mercy reaches deeper into our world.

In short

Being people of mercy means that we pay attention not to what we feel but what we do, and that we re-order our lives with actions of compassion and love.

For discussion

What can I do to bring about a change of atmosphere in my family or among my friends and colleagues at work where there has been a breakdown of trust?

What would be today's list of "seven corporal acts of mercy"?

Concluding Prayer

Jesus, lord of time,
Hold us in your eternity.
Jesus, image of God,
Travel with us the life of faith.
Jesus, friend of sinners,
Heal the brokenness of our world.
Jesus, lord of tomorrow,
Draw us into your future. Amen.

Sending Out

During this next week reflect on what you have learned and explored in this session. Think about those lists of deadly sins and heavenly virtues that we have discussed in this session, and about your own motives. How can you let God shape them so that you are more like Jesus?

These readings may help you in your reflections:

> The glory of God is a human being fully alive and the life of humanity is the vision of God.
>
> IRENAEUS (C. 130–C. 200)

> Abba Theodore of Pherme asked Abba Pambo, "Give me a word to live by." And with great reluctance he said to him, "Go, Theodore, and have compassion on all. Compassion allows us to speak freely to God."
>
> ABBA PAMBO (4TH CENTURY)

> The surest way of attaining to the love of God is to dwell on his mercies; the more we value them, the more we shall love God.
>
> FRANCIS DE SALES (1567–1622)

The service of the poor is to be preferred to all else and to be performed without delay. If at a time set aside for prayer, medicine or help has to be brought to some poor person, go and do what has to be done with an easy mind, offering it up to God as a prayer. God is not neglected if prayers are put aside in order that such work may be completed. Charity takes precedence over all rules. Everything ought to tend to it since it is itself a great lady: what it orders should be carried out. Let us show our service to the poor, then, with renewed ardor in our hearts, seeking out in particular any destitute people, since they are given to us as lords and patrons.

VINCENT DE PAUL (1581–1660)

God has made us to be like him. And what is this but to be holy? "Be ye holy, for I your God am holy." The mistake of mistakes is to think that holiness consists in great or extraordinary things beyond the reach of ordinary people. It has been well said, "Holiness does not consist in doing uncommon things, but in doing common things uncommonly well."

EDWARD BOUVERIE PUSEY (1800–82)

Holiness consists simply in doing the will of God and being just what God wants us to be.

THÉRÈSE OF LISIEUX (1873–97)

If you can't feed a hundred people, then just feed one.

MOTHER TERESA OF CALCUTTA (1910–97)

PEACEMAKING

pilgrim

In this session we look at what it means to be a peacemaker after the example of Christ and to recognize the cost of this witness. We start with some verses from Psalm 34 that speak of God's tender love towards those who are afflicted in the cause of peace.

Opening Prayers

Generous God, help me to live as a child of your kingdom
Give me the mind of Christ.

Let us hear our Lord's blessing on those who follow him.

"Blessed are the poor in spirit, for theirs is the kingdom of heaven.
"Blessed are those who mourn, for they will be comforted.
'"Blessed are the meek, for they will inherit the earth.
"Blessed are those who hunger and thirst for righteousness, for they
will be filled.
"Blessed are the merciful, for they will receive mercy.
"Blessed are the pure in heart, for they will see God.
"Blessed are the peacemakers, for they will be called children of God.
"Blessed are those who are persecuted for righteousness' sake, for
theirs is the kingdom of heaven."

MATTHEW 5:3-10

God of our days and years
We set this time apart for you.
Form us in the likeness of Christ
So that we may learn of your love
And that our lives may give you glory.
Amen.

Conversation

**Think of some people who you would call "peacemakers." What is it
about them that is so special?**

Reflecting on Scripture

Reading

Come, O children, listen to me;
I will teach you the fear of the Lord.
¹²Which of you desires life,
and covets many days to enjoy good?
¹³Keep your tongue from evil,
and your lips from speaking deceit.
¹⁴Depart from evil, and do good;
seek peace, and pursue it.

¹⁵The eyes of the Lord are on the righteous,
and his ears are open to their cry.
¹⁶The face of the Lord is against evildoers,
to cut off the remembrance of them from the earth.
¹⁷When the righteous cry for help, the Lord hears,
and rescues them from all their troubles.
¹⁸The Lord is near to the brokenhearted,
and saves the crushed in spirit.

¹⁹Many are the afflictions of the righteous,
but the Lord rescues them from them all.
²⁰He keeps all their bones;
not one of them will be broken.
²¹Evil brings death to the wicked,
and those who hate the righteous will be condemned.
²²The Lord redeems the life of his servants;
none of those who take refuge in him will be condemned.

PSALM 34:11-22

● Read the passage through once.

● Keep a few moments' silence.

● Read the passage a second time with different voices.

- Invite everyone to say aloud a word or phrase that strikes them.
- Read the passage a third time.
- Share together what this word or phrase might mean and what questions it raises.

Reflection   HELEN-ANN HARTLEY

"Blessed are the peacemakers...", "Blessed are those who are persecuted for righteousness' sake..."

Words like "peacemakers" and "persecuted" are familiar enough, but what do they really mean? It can seem difficult to unpack them from the midst of diverse contemporary political and social contexts. Part of the challenge of appreciating the richness and deep challenge that Jesus sets out in these verses lies in the invitation to learn from present day contexts where these words have urgent meaning. This is especially true of a word like "persecution," which in some parts of the world can literally be a matter of life or death. While not wishing to downgrade whatever our personal struggles might be of living out our faith openly wherever we are located, the knowledge that one of our sisters or brothers in Christ might face death because of their faith heightens the shocking nature of Jesus' statement that the reward of persecution is the kingdom of heaven. Future promise impacts on present vulnerability. Future reward gives hope for present troubles. With that, the command is to seek peace, for that is reflective of the very character of God.

The word that Matthew uses for "peacemakers" is worth noting because its Greek form in this verse is found nowhere else in the New Testament or in the Septuagint (the Greek translation of our Old Testament). It is significant because as a word it combines both an action as well as a reflection on the character of the action. It is as if Jesus is saying: "Blessed are those who seek peace peaceably." The emphasis on the manner of the action is important because that is where the real challenge lies. It is one thing to seek peace, but to attend to that seeking in a way that is utterly peaceful requires some effort, which becomes something of a virtue in itself. This is not to rule out the possibility of discord or even stronger than that, war, but the point seems to be that the distinctiveness of a Christian response might be known in the risk taken by seeking peace against the odds. In a first-century context where the Roman war machine was everywhere, this must have been shockingly challenging. But the surprises don't end there. The intentional peaceful search for peace enables the peacemaker to be reflective of God's very nature, which is both distinctive and transformative. Distinctive, because Christian discipleship constantly seeks to proclaim the particular good news of Jesus Christ, and transformative because that is the hallmark of the kingdom of heaven: everything is changed.

In short

Jesus calls us to "seek peace peaceably." This intentional peaceful search for peace reflects the deep character of God who also always and everywhere seeks for peace in the world.

For discussion

How do you understand the words "peacemaker" and "persecution"?

How should you be involved in making peace?

God's kingdom prevails

The eighth beatitude raises the topic of persecution, which in the context of the gospel might point to physical or verbal abuse. The type of persecution that is in mind here is brought on because of "righteousness." In other words, by doing God's will, persecution may follow. It is hard here not to reflect on the cross, even though there is perhaps surprisingly, no mention of it explicitly. By doing God's will, Jesus suffers and dies. But God's will points beyond that to the resurrection, which is part of the promised future glory that the kingdom of heaven entails. This future glory is what this beatitude presents in confident certainty. The verse is thick with meaning, however, and is rooted in elements in the Jewish wisdom tradition where the righteous individual is sought out, considered annoying, and thus disposed of. At the same time, the persistence of the righteous person delivers a signal that provokes thought and a desire to test the righteousness to see if it is truly of God.

The eighth beatitude also connects back to the first, linking both humility and persecution with the future promise of the kingdom. Both humility and resilience to persecution are seen as strengths, not weaknesses. We find the Beatitudes in Matthew's Gospel. The community he was writing for may themselves have known persecution. This suggests to us that whatever our present travails might be, we are neither the first to encounter a challenge nor the first to consider how to respond. Psalm 34:11-22 speaks powerfully of this when it celebrates the plight of the righteous and the saving power of God. The Beatitudes are ultimately about what happens when the realms of God and human beings connect and the kingdom of God prevails.

> **In short**
>
> Seeking righteousness may mean that we encounter persecution, but this reminds us of the cross and the fact that despite his own great suffering, Jesus rose again.

For discussion

- Can you think of some examples of peacemaking and of people being persecuted? (Are there things happening locally as well as nationally or globally?)

- How has following God's will brought you into situations of conflict?

- How have you responded?

Concluding Prayer

Jesus, lord of time,
Hold us in your eternity.
Jesus, image of God,
Travel with us the life of faith.
Jesus, friend of sinners,
Heal the brokenness of our world.
Jesus, lord of tomorrow,
Draw us into your future. Amen.

Sending Out

During this next week reflect on what you have learned and explored in this session. Think about being a peacemaker, and where it might lead. Are there situations you are facing at home or at work or in your neighborhood where someone needs to stand up for the cause of peace? Could you be that person? And what else should Christians be doing in the wider world to witness to God's peace?

These readings may help you in your reflections:

> God commands us to be peacemakers, to live in harmony, and to be of one mind in his house. We who are the children of God must make the peace of God a reality in our lives; we who share in the one Spirit must be of one heart and mind. God refuses the sacrifice of the quarrelsome, and instructs them to leave their gift before the altar, to go and be reconciled to their brother or sister. God is only pacified by prayer that is offered in a spirit of peace. So let our peace and fraternal harmony be the great sacrifice we offer God.
>
> CYPRIAN OF CARTHAGE (C. 200-58)

When the civil war in our nature has been brought to an end and we are at peace with ourselves, then we ourselves will become peace. Only then can we be true to the name of Christ that we bear.

GREGORY OF NYSSA (C. 330–94)

Just as there are many kinds of persecution, so there are many forms of martyrdom. You are a witness to Christ every day of your life.

AMBROSE OF MILAN (C. 334–97)

Let us not imprint on ourselves the image of a despot, but let Christ paint his image in us with his words: "My peace I give you, my peace I leave with you." The knowledge that peace is good is of no benefit if we do not practice it. The most valuable objects are invariably the most fragile; costly things require the most careful handling. Particularly fragile is that which is lost by gossip. People like nothing better than discussing and minding the business of others, passing on tittle-tattle and criticising people behind their backs. Those who cannot say: "The Lord has given me a discerning tongue, that I may with a word support those who are weary" should keep silent. Or if they must speak, then let them always promote peace.

COLUMBANUS (C. 543–615)

Our souls may lose their peace and even disturb other people's if we are always criticizing trivial actions which often are not real defects at all, but we construe them wrongly through our ignorance of their motives.

TERESA OF AVILA (1515–82)

Peace is not the absence of tension, but the presence of justice.

MARTIN LUTHER KING (1929–68)

What can you do to promote world peace? Go home and love your family.

MOTHER TERESA OF CALCUTTA (1910–97)

LIVING AS CITIZENS OF GOD'S KINGDOM

pilgrim

In this session we look at what Jesus meant by the kingdom and how we can live as its citizens. We start with Jesus telling us that we are called to be in the world like salt and light.

Opening Prayers

Generous God, help me to live as a child of your kingdom
Give me the mind of Christ.

Let us hear our Lord's blessing on those who follow him.

"Blessed are the poor in spirit, for theirs is the kingdom of heaven.
"Blessed are those who mourn, for they will be comforted.
"Blessed are the meek, for they will inherit the earth.
"Blessed are those who hunger and thirst for righteousness, for they will be filled.
"Blessed are the merciful, for they will receive mercy.
"Blessed are the pure in heart, for they will see God.
"Blessed are the peacemakers, for they will be called children of God.
"Blessed are those who are persecuted for righteousness' sake, for theirs is the kingdom of heaven."

MATTHEW 5:3-10

God of our days and years
We set this time apart for you.
Form us in the likeness of Christ
So that we may learn of your love
And that our lives may give you glory.
Amen.

Conversation

How much should the Christian faith influence our lives? Are there certain things that should be kept separate?

Reflecting on Scripture

Reading

"You are the salt of the earth; but if salt has lost its taste, how can its saltiness be restored? It is no longer good for anything, but is thrown out and trampled under foot. ¹⁴"You are the light of the world. A city built on a hill cannot be hidden. ¹⁵No one after lighting a lamp puts it under the bushel basket, but on the lampstand, and it gives light to all in the house. ¹⁶In the same way, let your light shine before others, so that they may see your good works and give glory to your Father in heaven. ¹⁷"Do not think that I have come to abolish the law or the prophets; I have come not to abolish but to fulfill. ¹⁸For truly I tell you, until heaven and earth pass away, not one letter, not one stroke of a letter, will pass from the law until all is accomplished. ¹⁹Therefore, whoever breaks one of the least of these commandments, and teaches others to do the same, will be called least in the kingdom of heaven; but whoever does them and teaches them will be called great in the kingdom of heaven."

MATTHEW 5:13-19

Explanatory note

Bushel basket: this was effectively a large bucket that could hold around 8 or so pounds of grain.

The law and the prophets may be just a general way of referring to the period that we now know as the Old Testament period or it may have the more specific meaning of referring to the first two collections of books in the Jewish ordering of what Christians call the Old Testament. The Jewish Bible is split into three main sections: the law, the prophets, and the writings.

Older translations translate a letter or stroke of a letter as "jot and tittle." The first word refers to the smallest consonant and the second word to the way of writing vowels in Hebrew. What this refers to is the smallest and apparently least important letter that you can write down.

- Read the passage through once.
- Keep a few moments' silence.
- Read the passage a second time with different voices.
- Invite everyone to say aloud a word or phrase that strikes them.
- Read the passage a third time.
- Share together what this word or phrase might mean and what questions it raises.

Reflection   EMMA INESON

Finding a home in the kingdom of God

Where do you live? Wherever it is, it's likely that you are living by the rules, expectations, and ways of doing things placed upon citizens of that society. When Jesus began his ministry he said that he had come to point the way to a new society or "kingdom." Anyone who lives by faith in Jesus is to be a citizen of this kingdom—the kingdom of God. This kingdom is not a geographical area, but a state of affairs, a way of living, an alternative reality, where God rules as king.

The Jewish people had long been looking for the day when injustice, oppression, and sorrow would be conquered, and when "the Lord will become king over all the earth," to quote the prophet Zechariah (14:9). So when Jesus began his ministry with the words, "The time is fulfilled, and the kingdom of God has come near; repent, and believe in the good news" (Mark 1:15), it's no wonder that he caused shockwaves. It could be said that the idea of the kingdom is the single most important concept in the New Testament. It's central to Jesus' teaching and the means by which we interpret everything he came to do. It is also crucial for understanding how Jesus' followers are to live, day-by-day. Becoming a citizen of the kingdom is remarkably simple. It's not by trying harder to keep all the rules. It's by turning towards Jesus in repentance that we come into God's kingdom. And it is free. In fact, Jesus takes a child as an example of what it means to enter this kingdom, someone who is poor in spirit.

So what kind of kingdom is it? Jesus' own disciples thought it might be a political or military kingdom, and were hoping for top jobs for themselves. But Jesus had a bigger agenda than getting rid of Caesar and the Roman imperialists; his agenda was to change human hearts, to bring people back to God, and to bring healing and reconciliation to the world (Matthew 19:28, Luke 4:16-19, 17:20, 21). It's an upside-down kingdom (or perhaps it's really the right way up, and the rest of the world is upside-down). The last will be first, the least will be greatest, and the meek will inherit everything.

So what does it mean to live in the kingdom? It means that as citizens we live according to God's principles of justice, peace, and love rather than the more natural human instincts of putting ourselves first. As citizens of the kingdom of God we commit ourselves to making God's kingdom a reality in the places where we live. Jesus announced the fact that God's kingdom was breaking into the world, but that process won't be complete until the end of time when God's rule is fully established on earth. In the meantime, as citizens of that kingdom, we set ourselves to make the kingdom present wherever and whenever we can. We should strive to bring out justice in the world we live in and to ensure that all people are treated with compassion and love as they would be in God's own kingdom.

> **In short**
>
> In his ministry Jesus announced that the kingdom of God was near and called his followers to live as citizens of this kingdom. This means that God's rule of justice and mercy is breaking into the world and we should live as though this is a reality.

For discussion

Share examples of when you have seen God's kingdom breaking into the kingdoms of the world.

How can you demonstrate and live by kingdom values in your home, your relationships, your work, your locality, your church?

Living by the values of God's kingdom

In his Sermon on the Mount Jesus tells us what a citizen of the kingdom should look like. As we have explored, the Beatitudes in particular describe the key blessings and promises of the kingdom and the character of its citizens: humility, dependence on God's comfort, gentleness, hunger for the right ways of God, mercy towards others, purity in motive and deed, a passion for peace, and willingness to face opposition, even persecution, for his sake. The Beatitudes have been called the "great reversal," because they describe a stark alternative to the realities of this world, where all too often might is right and the rich inherit everything. The kingdom is, in some respects, a subversive movement, and Christians will feel the jarring contrast between living in human society, and their citizenship of the kingdom of heaven. That's why Jesus calls us to be "salt" and "light" to those around.

There are many "kingdoms" in the world—political, financial, economic, social, and others. Citizens of the kingdom of heaven, Christians, will daily seek to live out the reality of God's reign increasingly in their lives and in the world around them. This does not always need to be in dramatic ways (although it might be); Jesus described the kingdom using images of small things: mustard seeds, yeast in dough, a lost coin. But it does need to be an intentional choice to live according to the ways of God's kingdom. Jesus calls us to "seek first the kingdom" and to pray that it comes "on earth as it is in heaven."

> **In short**
> As citizens of God's kingdom we are called to live by values marked by God's reign. The Beatitudes summarize what these values are.

For discussion

- What does being a "citizen of the kingdom" mean for you? And what are the biggest challenges?

- How do you see the Beatitudes changing lives for those committed to kingdom principles?

Concluding Prayer

Jesus, lord of time,
Hold us in your eternity.
Jesus, image of God,
Travel with us the life of faith.
Jesus, friend of sinners,
Heal the brokenness of our world.
Jesus, lord of tomorrow,
Draw us into your future. Amen.

Sending Out

During this next week reflect on what you have learned and explored in this session. Think about the kingdom of God and how you can live as one of its citizens this week. Will others notice anything? How might you expect them to observe any difference? Not just in the way you deal with them, but in other decisions you make? How you spend your money? How you use your time? What you give your energy to?

These readings may help you in your reflections:

Christians are not distinguishable from other people by nationality or language or the way they dress. They do not live in cities reserved to themselves; they do not speak a special dialect; there is nothing eccentric about their way of life. Their beliefs are not the invention of some sharp, inquisitive mind, nor are they like some, slaves of this or that school of thought. They are distributed among Greek and non-Greek cities alike, according to their human lot. They conform to local usage in their dress, diet, and manner of life. Nevertheless, in their communities they do reveal some extraordinary and undeniably paradoxical attitudes. They live each in his or her own native country, but they are like pilgrims in transit. They play their full part as citizens and are content to submit to every burden as if they were resident aliens. For them, every foreign country is home, and every homeland is foreign territory… In a word, what the soul is to the body, Christians are to the world.

LETTER TO DIOGNETUS (C. 150)

Dear friends, what can be more delightful than this voice of the Lord inviting us? See, in his loving mercy, the Lord is showing us the way of life. Clothed with faith and the performance of good works, and with the gospel as our guide, let us set out on this way of life so that we may deserve to see God who is calling us into his kingdom.

BENEDICT (480–550)

Amid the tumult of outward cares, inwardly a great peace and calm is reigning in love.

GREGORY THE GREAT (540–604)

Let nothing disturb you,
Let nothing frighten you.
All things pass away:
God never changes.
Patience obtains all things.
Those who have God lack nothing:
God alone suffices.

TERESA OF ÁVILA (1515–82)

The kingdom is something within you which has the power of growth like a seed; something that you discover almost accidentally; something that you are searching for and of whose value you become more confident and excited as the search proceeds, and you discover truer, lovelier things which are constantly being surpassed; something for which you have to give everything you have, no less yet no more, including the earlier finds with which you were once so completely delighted.

GEORGE APPLETON (1902–93)

SESSION SIX:
FOUNDATIONS

pilgrim

In this session we look at what it means to build your whole life on the teaching and example of Jesus as we have seen this in the Beatitudes. We start with one of Jesus' most famous stories comparing someone who built their house on rock to someone who built their house on sand.

Opening Prayers

Generous God, help me to live as a child of your kingdom
Give me the mind of Christ.

Let us hear our Lord's blessing on those who follow him.

"Blessed are the poor in spirit, for theirs is the kingdom of heaven.
"Blessed are those who mourn, for they will be comforted.
"Blessed are the meek, for they will inherit the earth.
"Blessed are those who hunger and thirst for righteousness, for they will be filled.
"Blessed are the merciful, for they will receive mercy.
"Blessed are the pure in heart, for they will see God.
"Blessed are the peacemakers, for they will be called children of God.
"Blessed are those who are persecuted for righteousness' sake, for theirs is the kingdom of heaven."

MATTHEW 5:3-10

God of our days and years
We set this time apart for you.
Form us in the likeness of Christ
So that we may learn of your love
And that our lives may give you glory.
Amen.

Conversation

What makes you truly happy?

Reflecting on Scripture

Reading

[Jesus said] "Everyone then who hears these words of mine and acts on them will be like a wise man who built his house on rock. ²⁵The rain fell, the floods came, and the winds blew and beat on that house, but it did not fall, because it had been founded on rock. ²⁶And everyone who hears these words of mine and does not act on them will be like a foolish man who built his house on sand. ²⁷The rain fell, and the floods came, and the winds blew and beat against that house, and it fell—and great was its fall!" ²⁸Now when Jesus had finished saying these things, the crowds were astounded at his teaching, ²⁹for he taught them as one having authority, and not as their scribes.

MATTHEW 7:24-29

- Read the passage through once.
- Keep a few moments' silence.
- Read the passage a second time with different voices.
- Invite everyone to say aloud a word or phrase that strikes them.
- Read the passage a third time.
- Share together what this word or phrase might mean and what questions it raises.

Reflection   MARTIN WARNER

The "behappytudes"

The Jerusalem Bible, published in 1966, was among the first to translate ancient Hebrew and Greek biblical texts into modern English. One of the startling innovations (for those familiar with the Bible) was the substitution of the word "happy" for the word "blessed" in the translation of the Beatitudes.

The Jerusalem Bible translators seem to be prompting us to find a richer meaning in the term "happy" than our everyday usage might convey. What is the scope of that richer meaning?

First, the Bible suggests that authentic happiness (the sense of being blessed) cannot be seized as a right but is more naturally experienced as a gift. This begins to emerge early in the Old Testament, in a family situation with its potential for rivalry and friction.

At the end of Genesis, Israel, the father of Joseph the dreamer, blesses Joseph's two boys before he dies. Israel crosses his hands, so that the younger is given symbolic priority by being blessed with the right hand, the older with the left hand. Joseph is irritated with his father and tries to reassert the order of nature, but the frail old man refuses.

As his life draws to a close, Israel, known originally as Jacob, remembers that he was the younger and more disreputable of two brothers, and yet he slowly became the one in whom beatitude—happiness—was received from God in extraordinary ways.

This tiny detail in the early pages of the Old Testament finds a powerful echo in the letters of Paul in the New Testament: "But God chose what is foolish in the world to shame the wise; God chose what is weak in the world to shame the strong" (1 Corinthians 1:27).

Happiness, in the experience of Jacob and of Paul, is not a fatalistic acceptance of things they cannot change: rather, it is the acceptance of God's transforming love, offered to them as a gift.

In short

True happiness—or the experience of knowing yourself to be blessed—is not a right but something that is given to us by God as a gift.

For discussion

- The Jerusalem Bible suggests "happy" as an alternative to "blessed"—how does this change your understanding of what happiness is?

- Can you think of examples of when you have found happiness in life not by getting what you wanted, nor by grimly just accepting things as they are, but by finding God's love revealed in the ups and downs of life as it is?

Delighting in God

Happiness is also intimately bound up with a capacity for worship—the heart's response to God's creativity, the dignity of saying, "Thank you."

In the Psalms, the hymnbook of the Old Testament, the first word of the first psalm is "blessed"—or "happy" in some modern translations. This psalm invites us into the worship of God and takes us deeper. First we are told that to live God's way is to be like "trees planted by living water, which yield their fruit in due season" (Psalm 1:3). We explored this image in Session One, when we thought about the fruits that grow naturally from that poverty of spirit which means great openness to God. It is in contemplation and worship that we root ourselves in this way. We find "delight in the law of the Lord." This reference to law is not about institutional regulation, but a patient fascination with the way things lead us to God and what such things might be.

This calls to mind those people who have a serenity about them, emerging from the stillness within themselves and symptomatic of seeking to know what God is like. They are ordinary people of every kind who have developed the profound capacity God gives each of us for worship with others and for prayer in stillness and simplicity.

This dimension of the Beatitudes turns our attention to the character and quality of the worship in our churches. Does it create an appetite for daily personal delight in the law of the Lord? Or might our liturgy be too busy and self-important to nurture the serenity of discovering the ways of God?

Finally, happiness resides in the sense that we are more than finite creatures. The Beatitudes form an agenda whereby Jesus outlines for us what transition into the vision of God might be like.

These eight-fold couplets of endeavor and fulfillment begin to mark out what the quality of that vision will be like. They are the rock, the sure foundation upon which Christian lives are built. It is therefore no accident that they are the Gospel reading on All Saints' Day, celebrating the holy souls who enjoy happiness perfected in resurrection life.

The Beatitudes are often the set reading for a funeral, especially if there is to be a Eucharist. Here, in liturgical re-enactment, Jesus promises the gift of resurrection and immortality to his brother or sister resting in death, saying, "*Yours* is the kingdom of heaven."

Augustine of Hippo (354–430) wrote, towards the end of his life, that "many despair of being immortal, though no one can be happy without this. By failing to believe that they could be immortal they fail to live so that they can be." Like the translators of the Jerusalem Bible, Augustine understood happiness to be so serious and profound a quality that it could describe the very nature of God—"the best and happiest spirit of all."

May the Beatitudes inspire you to discover in time the dynamics of God's eternal happiness.

> ### In short
> The Beatitudes point us to the sure foundations upon which Christian lives can be built, and remind us that happiness lies in responding to the love that God shows us.

For discussion

- Having now studied the Beatitudes at some depth, which of them do you find most appealing and which most challenging?
- How do you see them lived out in Jesus' own life?
- How do you think they are going to change you?
- How might they lead you to greater happiness?

Concluding Prayer

Jesus, lord of time,
Hold us in your eternity.
Jesus, image of God,
Travel with us the life of faith.
Jesus, friend of sinners,
Heal the brokenness of our world.
Jesus, lord of tomorrow,
Draw us into your future. Amen.

Sending Out

During this next week reflect on what you have learned and explored in this session. Think about how happiness is found in seeing God in everyday things; in worship; and in allowing ourselves to be transformed—to receive the promises of the Beatitudes. Pay attention to ordinary things this week and to the possibility of disclosing God. And attend worship with an increased expectation that God will meet you and serve you. Most of all, be thankful and express that gratitude to others.

These readings may help you in your reflections:

Great endeavors and hard struggles await those who are converted,
but afterwards inexpressible joy. If you want to light a fire, you are
troubled at first by smoke and your eyes water. But in the end you
achieve your aim. Now it is written, "Our God is a consuming fire."
So we must light the divine fire in us with tears and struggles.

AMMA SYNCLETICA (4TH CENTURY)

Christ is with me, whom then shall I fear? Let the waves rise up
against me, the seas, the wrath of rulers: these things to me are
mere cobwebs. I always say, "Lord, your will be done"; not what this
person or that person wishes, but as you wish. This is my fortress,
this is my immovable rock, this is my firm staff.

JOHN CHRYSOSTOM (347–407)

God is working in us, helping us to thank and trust and enjoy him.
It is the meaning of those sweet and cheering words he spoke to me
when he said, "I am the foundation of your praying."

JULIAN OF NORWICH (1373–1417)

Keep me, O Lord, while I tarry on this earth, in a daily serious
seeking after thee and in a believing affectionate walking with thee;
that when thou comest, I may be found not hiding my talent, nor
yet asleep with my lamp unfurnished; but waiting and longing for
my Lord, my glorious God.

RICHARD BAXTER (1615–91)

The spiritual life is impoverished and stunted because we give
so little place to gratitude. It is more important to thank God
for blessings received than to pray for them beforehand. For
that forward looking prayer, though right as an expression of
dependence upon God, is still self-centered in part, at least, in its
interest; there is something which we hope to gain by our prayer.
The backward-looking act of thanksgiving is free from this. It is
quite selfless. It is akin to love. All our love to God is in response to
his love for us. (1 John 4:19)

WILLIAM TEMPLE (1881–1944)

I am not sure exactly what heaven will be like, but I know that when we die and it comes time for God to judge us, he will not ask, "How many good things have you done in your life?" Rather he will ask, "How much love did you put into what you did?"

MOTHER TERESA OF CALCUTTA (1910–97)

NOTES

New Patterns for Worship, London, Church House Publishing, 2002:
Opening Prayer (all sessions) (from p. 397).
Concluding Prayer (all sessions) (from p. 291).

Introduction to the Beatitudes
Robert Warren, *Living Well: The Archbishop of Canterbury's Lent Book*, London, Fount, 1998.

Session One
Bernard of Clairvaux (1090–1153), *Sermon on the Song of Songs*, XVIII, 2, 3.
Francis de Sales (1567–1622), *Introduction to the Devout Life*, I, 2.
Hilary of Poitiers (315–67), *On the Trinity*, I, 1.
Hildegard of Bingen (1098–1179), *Letter to the Abbot of Ebrach*.
Thomas Merton (1915–68), *New Seeds of Contemplation*, London, Burns & Oates, 1961, p. 24 © Thomas Merton Legacy Trust.

Session Two
Benedict (480–550), from the Prologue to the *Rule*.
Maria Boulding (1929–2009), *Gateway to Hope*, London, Fount, 1985, p. 110.
Thomas Merton (1915–68), *Thoughts in Solitude*, London, Burns & Oates, p. 85 © Thomas Merton Legacy Trust.
Metropolitan Anthony of Sourozh (1914–2003), *God and Man*, London, Darton, Longman and Todd, 1971.
John Henry Newman (1801–90), *Plain and Parochial Sermons*, London, 1939, vol. 4, p. 378.
Teresa of Avila (1515–82), *The Way of Perfection*, 32.

Session Three
Abba Pambo (4th century), *Sayings of the Desert Fathers and Mothers*, 14.
Edward Bouverie Pusey (1800–82), Sermon 12 "Saintliness of Christians," *Parochial and Cathedral Sermons*, Oxford, 1882, p. 167.
Vincent de Paul (1581–1660), Letter 2546.
Francis de Sales (1567–1622), *Introduction to the Devout Life*, III, 5.
Irenaeus (*c*. 130–*c*. 200), *Against Heresies*, IV, 20, 5.
Mother Teresa of Calcutta (1910–97).
Thérèse of Lisieux (1873–97), *Collected Letters of Thérèse of Lisieux*.

Session Four
Ambrose of Milan (*c*. 334–97), *Exposition of Psalm 118*, 20, 47.
Columbanus (*c*. 543–615), *Instructions*, 11, 2.
Cyprian of Carthage (*c*. 200–58), *On the Lord's Prayer*, 23.
Gregory of Nyssa (*c*. 330–94), *On Christian Perfection*.
Martin Luther King (1929–68).

Mother Teresa of Calcutta (1910–97).
Teresa of Avila (1515–82), *Interior Castle*, 2.

Session Five
George Appleton (1902–93), *Journey for a Soul*, London, Collins, 1976, p. 160.
Benedict (480–550), from the Prologue to *Rule*.
Gregory the Great (540–604), *Commentary on the Book of Job*, 18, 43, 70.
Letter to Diognetus (c. 150), 5.
Teresa of Avila (1515–82), *Poem IX: Exclamations of the Soul to God*.

Session Six
Amma Syncletica (4th century), *Sayings of the Desert Fathers and Mothers*.
Richard Baxter (1615–91), *The Reformed Pastor.*
John Chrysostom (347–407), *Homily before his Exile*, 2.
Julian of Norwich (1373–1417), *Revelations of Divine Love*, 86.
William Temple (1881–1944), *Readings in St John's Gospel*, London, Macmillan & Co., 1947, p. 189.
Mother Teresa of Calcutta (1910–97).